973.8 Col

P9-DEE-338

The RISE
of INDUSTRY

1860–1900

★ ★ The Drama of AMERICAN HISTORY ★ ★

The RISE
of INDUSTRY

1860–1900

Christopher Collier
James Lincoln Collier

BENCHMARK BOOKS

MARSHALL CAVENDISH
NEW YORK

ACKNOWLEDGMENT: The authors wish to thank Walter Licht, Professor of History and Director of the Graduate Division, University of Pennsylvania, for his careful reading of the text of this volume in The Drama of American History series and his thoughtful and useful comments. The work has been much improved by Professor Licht's notes. The authors are deeply in his debt, but, of course, assume full responsibility for the substance of the work, including any errors that may appear.

Photo research by James Lincoln Collier.
COVER PHOTO: © Joslyn Art Museum
PICTURE CREDITS: The photographs in this book are used by permission and through the courtesy of :
Abby Aldrich Rockefeller Folk Art Center, Williamsburg: 10 (top), 10 (bottom). Joslyn Art Museum, Omaha, Nebraska: 11. Corbis-Bettmann: 13, 14, 19, 24, 25, 27, 28, 39, 45, 46, 55 (top), 57, 58, 65, 66, 69, 70, 72, 74, 77, 82 (right). Independence National Historical Park: 21 (top), 21 (bottom).
Museum of the City of New York: 42, 49, 52, 53, 55 (bottom).

Benchmark Books
Marshall Cavendish Corporation
99 White Plains Road
Tarrytown, New York 10591-9001

©2000 Christopher Collier and James Lincoln Collier

Library of Congress Cataloging-in-Publication Data

Collier, Christopher, date
The rise of industry : 1860-1900 / Christopher Collier, James Lincoln Collier.
p. cm. — (The drama of American history)
Includes bibliographical references and index.
Summary: Describes the period after the Civil War when the United States was becoming increasingly industrialized and technological, including the coming of the railroads, the rise of the large corporations, the development of labor unions, and government regulation.
ISBN 0-7614-0820-7
1. Industries—United States—History—19th century—Juvenile literature. 2. Manufacturing industries—United States—History—19th century—Juvenile literature. 3. Technology—United States —History—19th century—Juvenile literature 4. United States—Economic conditions—1865-1918 —Juvenile literature.
[1. Industries—History. 2. Technology—History. 3. United States—Economic conditions—1865-1918.]
I. Collier, James Lincoln, date. II. Title. III. Series: Collier, Christopher, date Drama of American history.
HC105. 7.C65 2000
338.0973'09'034—dc21   98-38528
                                                                                                           CIP
                                                                                                           AC

Printed in Italy

1 3 5 6 4 2

CONTENTS

Over many years of both teaching and writing for students at all levels, from grammar school to graduate school, it has been borne in on us that many, if not most, American history textbooks suffer from trying to include everything of any moment in the history of the nation. Students become lost in a swamp of factual information, and as a consequence lose track of how those facts fit together and why they are significant and relevant to the world today.

In this series, our effort has been to strip the vast amount of available detail down to a central core. Our aim is to draw in bold strokes, providing enough information, but no more than is necessary, to bring out the basic themes of the American story, and what they mean to us now. We believe that it is surely more important for students to grasp the underlying concepts and ideas that emerge from the movement of history, than to memorize an array of facts and figures.

The difference between this series and many standard texts lies in what has been left out. We are convinced that students will better remember the important themes if they are not buried under a heap of names, dates, and places.

In this sense, our primary goal is what might be called citizenship education. We think it is critically important for America as a nation and Americans as individuals to understand the origins and workings of the public institutions that are central to American society. We have asked ourselves again and again what is most important for citizens of our democracy to know so they can most effectively make the system work for them and the nation. For this reason, we have focused on political and institutional history, leaving social and cultural history less well developed.

This series is divided into volumes that move chronologically through the American story. Each is built around a single topic, such as the Pilgrims, the Constitutional Convention, or immigration. Each volume has been written so that it can stand alone, for students who wish to research a given topic. As a consequence, in many cases material from previous volumes is repeated, usually in abbreviated form, to set the topic in its historical context. That is to say, students of the Constitutional Convention must be given some idea of relations with England, and why the Revolution was fought, even though the material was covered in detail in a previous volume. Readers should find that each volume tells an entire story that can be read with or without reference to other volumes.

Despite our belief that it is of the first importance to outline sharply basic concepts and generalizations, we have not neglected the great dramas of American history. The stories that will hold the attention of students are here, and we believe they will help the concepts they illustrate to stick in their minds. We think, for example, that knowing of Abraham Baldwin's brave and dramatic decision to vote with the small states at the Constitutional Convention will bring alive the Connecticut Compromise, out of which grew the American Senate.

Each of these volumes has been read by esteemed specialists in its particular topic; we have benefited from their comments.

CHAPTER I

The Power of Technology

In the history of the United States the period from about 1870, when the country was settling down after the Civil War, to about 1900 was a time of immense change—quite possibly the most dynamic era in the nation's life. When the period began, America was still largely a rural country. Nearly three-quarters of Americans lived on farms or in small agricultural communities. A lot of clothing was store-bought, but most other things of daily use were still made at home. Bread, pies, and cakes were baked in coal or wood stoves. Most people's milk came from pails, not bottles. Bathwater was drawn from wells in wooden buckets and heated on stoves—but not very often. Music came from parlor pianos and crude fiddles, rather than from machines. In 1870 work for most people meant physical labor outdoors, plowing fields with oxen and mules, cutting hay with scythes, felling trees with axes and handsaws, mining coal with picks and shovels, catching fish with nets and lines from open dories. About 15 percent of the nation's women worked in mills or as servants in the houses of the well-to-do, but the rest spent twelve or fourteen hours a day working in their homes, shelling peas, washing clothes in buckets and ironing them with flatirons heated on stoves, milk-

Above, a well-known folk painting of a quilting party, where people gathered to enjoy themselves as they worked on quilts. At right, a portion of an elaborate quilt. The design was carefully sewn in stitch by stitch. Homemade goods were usually quite rough, but they could be elegant, as this quilt was.

In the mid-1800s the majority of Americans lived on farms or in small towns, like New Harmony, Indiana, using horses or their own feet for transportation, and rarely going more than a few miles from their own homes.

ing cows, feeding chickens in the backyard and weeding carrots and lettuce in the kitchen garden—and, of course, taking care of children.

By 1900 this rather cozy, if hard, world of rural America had all but disappeared. In its place was a busy, dynamic society built around cities and vast new industrial machines, the largest in the world. In 1900 almost half of Americans lived in cities, not on farms. In 1900 Americans were increasingly making their livings in mills and factories, doing repetitive jobs, rather than outdoor farmwork. Americans in 1900 found in the stores and shops around them an immense amount of ready-made goods. These millions of city dwellers did not milk cows, preserve their own jelly and pickles, bake bread, butcher hogs: Instead these processes were done in often distant factories and the products sold in local retail stores.

The basis for the modern America we know today had arrived. There were still no televisions, no airplanes, and only the most experimental automobiles. But the cities where so many Americans now lived were much like they are today: In fact, many of the apartment buildings where Americans live in 2000, many of the buildings where they work, were going up in the years around 1900.

This book tells the story of how, in two short generations, the American economy—and much of society—was remade.

It is obvious that inventions, new ways of doing things, can have great consequences for a society: The invention of the steam engine, for example, made possible steam-driven factories, steamships, and railroads. The application of such new ideas to industry, and life in general, is called *technology*. In recent decades we have seen technologies like electronics and computers dramatically change how people work, play, and communicate. But the technological changes that have taken place recently pale in comparison with those of the second half of the nineteenth century. It is probable that never in human history has there been such great technological change as came in the decades after the Civil War. A person born at the close of that war found himself as an adult living in a world very different from the one he had grown up in.

Indeed, the modern American industrial system began with the creation of the textile industry. Until about 1810 most clothing was made by hand. Housewives spun cotton or wool into yarn, wove it into cloth, cut and sewed the cloth into pants, skirts, and shirts. Wealthy people bought cloth and had their clothes made by tailors, but these were the few: The bulk of Americans wore clothes made at home. By the late 1820s machines for spinning fiber into yarn and weaving yarn into cloth, largely developed in England, were turning out much better cloth than most housewives could make; as time went on, other machines were developed to cut and sew cloth and to make clothes in factories. Taken together, these mills for spinning, weaving, and making clothing formed a huge textile and garment industry. Many of the businessmen who started these spinning and weaving mills—most of them in New England—got rich.

The textile industry by itself was not big enough to change America. For one thing, the factories at first depended on water power, which meant that they usually had to be built in the countryside next to a river or stream. But it showed people what industrialization could do.

Of course, mills of all sorts—for sawing logs into lumber, grinding wheat and corn into flour, for cleaning homespun wool fabric, and scores of other processes—were scattered across the American countryside by the thousands during the eighteenth century. But the modern factory system did not begin until Samuel Slater, in 1790, constructed the first real factory, in Pawtucket, Rhode Island—a building where several of the processes for making textiles were all contained under one roof, powered by a single water-wheel system.

It was the development of the steam engine that freed industrialists from the dependence on the waterpower that had kept their factories har-

The first true industry in the United States was textiles, made up of factories that spun wool or cotton into thread, and then wove the thread into cloth by machine. This picture shows a spinning mill, in which cotton is being spun into yarn, or thread. Many young women came off the farms to work in such mills.

nessed to inland streams and rivers. Steam was critically important to changing that world. The principle of steam power dates to ancient days, but the modern steam engine was developed in England in the late 1700s. In 1787 an American, John Fitch, invented a steamboat. It was not very successful, but in 1807 Robert Fulton devised an improved version, and very quickly steamboats appeared everywhere, substantially speeding up traffic on rivers, canals, and along the Atlantic and Gulf Coasts. Soon steam was applied to oceangoing vessels. Freed of dependence on wind and weather, steamships reduced the Atlantic crossing from weeks, or even months, to two weeks and eventually to a week. (The transportation revolution is discussed in more detail in the volume of "The Drama of American History" called *Andrew Jackson's America*.)

Businessmen quickly saw that the steam engine could be used to power machinery in factories, and over just two or three decades factories powered by the steam engine replaced most of the old waterpowered mills. This technological change also made sweeping changes in

Steam power brought the first technological revolution. John Fitch's rudimentary steamboat used a steam engine to move oars that pushed the boat through the water.

American life. Factories that ran on waterpower had to be located near streams or rivers in the countryside, and thus had a problem in finding workers. In Lowell, Massachusetts, hundreds of young women were brought to the mills and housed in dormitories nearby. In Oxford, Massachusetts, Samuel Slater created a town around his mills, with houses, shops, and schools for his workers. In Derby, Connecticut, mill owner David Humphreys built huge dormitories to house orphan boys brought in from New York City.

Perhaps even more important, a factory in the countryside had a lot of transportation problems, for raw material had to be carted in somehow, and finished goods carted out; and streams good for power are usually not so good for transportation—and, of course, they often froze up in winter.

The *steam*-powered factory, however, could be located in the middle of a city, where there was good transportation, and plenty of workers living within walking distance. The ideal situation was the port city with good railroad connections, providing both rail and ship transportation. It is not an accident that cities like New York and Philadelphia were among the first to become industrialized.

In the creation of the American industrial system, everything was tied to everything else. The new steam-powered factories needed immense amounts of coal to heat the boilers, and so the coal industry boomed. Coal needed railroads with powerful engines to tug long trains of cars, and strong rails to bear all that weight. These engines, and the rails they ran on, had to be made of high-quality steel. And fortunately for the industrial system, just at the right moment there came along a new technology for producing large quantities of high-quality steel.

Steel, which is made by heating iron in a certain way and adding small amounts of other elements, had been known for centuries, but it was very difficult to make because of the high temperatures required, and could only be made in small batches. Henry Bessemer, in England, discovered that if a stream of air was blown through molten ore, the oxygen in the air would actually ignite the carbon impurities in the iron, which would not only burn away but in burning would produce enough heat to turn the iron to steel. (An American, William Kelly, had discovered this process about ten years earlier, but did not patent or publicize it.) By 1856 Bessemer had perfected the system, and soon Bessemer steel was being turned out in massive quantities. Entrepreneurs soon saw that steel was far better than wood or iron for bridges and trestles carrying freight trains loaded with coal and ore. In the decades after the Civil War, Andrew Carnegie and other wealthy American entrepreneurs, aware that the railroads alone would be a tremendous market for steel, invested huge sums to build great steel mills.

Steel was gobbled up as fast as it could be produced. In 1875 about 157,000 tons of steel were produced in the United States; by 1910 it was 26 million tons. New techniques and quantity production drove prices down from $50 a ton for rails in 1875 to $18 a ton in the 1890s. We can thus see how closely bound the whole system was: The iron ore and coal the steel mills used in such enormous quantities had to be carried on rails in cars made of the very steel that the mills were producing.

As important as steel to our modern industrial system is oil, especially the gasoline produced from it. Without oil there would be no internal combustion engine, which drives our cars and trucks, many boats, airplanes, and other machines. Jet engines, too, burn fuel made from oil. In the early nineteenth century, whale oil, burned in saucerlike lamps, was widely used for lighting. Other types of oil produced from coal began to come into use in the 1800s. There was also a type of oil that seeped out of the ground in places. This oil, too, could be burned in lamps, but it was mostly used in patent medicines to treat a variety of diseases (needless to say, it did not cure much, if anything).

Then in 1859, just as the Bessemer steel process was being worked out, in Titusville, Pennsylvania, Edwin L. Drake drilled the first oil well. At sixty-nine feet he hit oil. Within weeks thousands of other people, determined to get rich on oil, flocked into the area and began setting up oil wells, and by 1862 oil production, mostly in Pennsylvania, was more than 100 million gallons a year. Rapidly improved methods of refining oil into kerosene were developed; and lamps, and in time, heaters and stoves, were invented to burn it. The oil industry overproduced during these early days, thus keeping prices low, but fortunes could be made: The Rockefeller fortune was originally based on oil. But of course the real importance of oil was as refined into gasoline for use in the internal combustion engine, which did not achieve prominence until the twentieth century.

Technology was transforming communication as well as transportation. Americans had always had to depend upon the mails to exchange information, and in a nation cut with poor roads, and slow-moving boats and ships, it took days, and sometimes weeks, for letters to get from one distant city to another. With the railroads, the mail speeded up, but even so it could take days for a letter to go long distances. Then, in 1844, Samuel F. B. Morse built, with government aid, the first experimental telegraph line. The telegraph was a scheme for sending a series of electrical impulses along wires so that when a telegraph operator pressed a key at one end of the line, a key at the other end would buzz. By means of combinations of short and long buzzes, known as the Morse code, a good operator could send or receive many words a minute. Within a few years, technical difficulties had been ironed out, and telegraph lines were being flung across the country, to connect cities, towns, and villages, just as the rails had connected them. Indeed, telegraph wires were often strung along railroad lines, where there were already rights-of-way.

This new communications system was immensely important to business. It allowed, for example, a textile manufacturer in Boston to get the latest prices of cotton in New Orleans and place an order within minutes. It also changed American newspapers, for now editors in Boston and Cincinnati could get the story of a fire in San Francisco or a shipwreck off

Charleston overnight, and have it on the front page the next morning. Railroad engineers and managers, too, welcomed the telegraph, for it allowed them to find out exactly where their trains were at any moment. The telegraph was a significant factor in the Civil War, for with it, instead of depending on a messenger on horseback, a general could learn of enemy movements and order reinforcements or supplies almost instantly.

Communication was further improved in 1876 when Alexander Graham Bell first patented his invention, the telephone. Within a year phones were being installed in thousands of offices and many homes. Quickly the new device spread, and by 1884 long-distance telephone lines were allowing people to make calls from city to city.

The telegraph and telephone were both dependent upon a revolution in electric power. The phenomenon of electricity had attracted the attention of scientists like Benjamin Franklin in the 1700s, and a good deal of progress in understanding its principles had been made. About one hundred and thirty years after Franklin's laboratory experiments, Thomas Alva Edison developed the incandescent lightbulb, the ancestor of the one we use today; by 1881 he was supplying customers with electric light.

But there remained problems with sending electricity in quantity over long distances. In the 1890s an inventor named George Westinghouse learned that some French experimenters had discovered a process by which electricity could be sent longer distances, known as *alternating current*. Westinghouse bought American rights to the process, and soon was sending alternating current to light four hundred lamps in a building in Lawrenceville, a suburb of Pittsburgh, from a dynamo four miles away. It was now possible to light homes cheaply with electricity, and by 1900 kerosene and gas lamps were going the way of the hand loom and the spinning wheel.

Perhaps even more important than the use of electricity for light was its application to motors. It was clear that machines powered by electricity would be a vast improvement over steam power. Steam required

Thomas Alva Edison was the most famous American inventor of his day, contributing to the development of electricity, sound recording, and the movie projector. Here we see him with an early phonograph, the forerunner of today's sophisticated recording systems.

separate belts and chains running from a wheel at a central steam engine through a factory to power each machine. With electricity, each machine could have its own motor. In the 1870s a number of scientists, especially Nikola Tesla, in Edison's laboratories, worked out a practical electric motor, and in 1882 Edison installed in New York City a central dynamo that could deliver power to surrounding homes and factories. Electric power developed rapidly thereafter, in time supplanting steam power in most mills and factories.

These inventions, which so rapidly changed American life, did not always spring out of an inventor's head. Usually they were developed over time, step-by-step, in hundreds, even thousands, of small improvements by many scientists, inventors, even imaginative youths working in small machine shops in little towns. One such man was George

Westinghouse. He was born in a little town in upstate New York in 1846. His father had a small machine shop, where he made a type of threshing machine. (A threshing machine separates the grain from the stems and husks of wheat and other seed plants.) George spent much of his youth in the machine shop. After serving in both the Army and the Navy in the Civil War, Westinghouse returned to his father's shop. When he was only nineteen he patented his first invention—a small steam engine.

When he was twenty, he happened to see a train wreck, in which cars had been derailed. As he watched the workmen trying to put the cars back on the rails, it occurred to him that there must be a more efficient way of doing it. He went home and sat up all night working out a new scheme. At first nobody would invest money to make his invention. But he persisted and eventually got backing. His "car-replacer" proved successful and his career was started.

He now turned his mind to other problems facing the new railroad industry, and invented several other devices to improve the efficiency of trains. Once, a train he was riding on was held up by a collision of two other trains farther along the line. The engineers of the trains involved in the wreck had seen each other when they were still some distance apart, and had blown their warning whistles. At that time the brakes on each car had to be screwed down separately by brakemen, and they had not been able to stop the trains quickly enough.

Westinghouse realized that a better braking system would save many lives and money. He learned about some French engineers who were drilling a tunnel in Italy using air-pressure drills. He immediately realized that air pressure was the answer to the brake problem, for air pressure could be delivered almost instantly to all the cars in a train at the same time. Once again he had trouble getting financing for his invention: Several wealthy financiers quickly and curtly ordered him out of their offices. But eventually Westinghouse got a chance to try out his system on a test train with an engine and four passenger cars. Shortly after the

The extent to which America—and the world—changed during the 1800s is shown in these two pictures. Top, a view of Second Street, Philadelphia, around 1800. Bottom, modern Philadelphia.

test train left the station, a wagon got stuck on the tracks directly in front of it. The engineer slammed on the new air brakes, and the train stopped four feet from the driver of the wagon. Westinghouse's invention was proven.

Westinghouse continued to work at devices for railroads. His interest in developing electrical signaling equipment led him into studying electricity generally. In time he developed the alternating current system, and built up the huge manufacturing concern that today bears his name.

George Westinghouse was typical of many men of his time. He was clever, hardworking, persistent, determined to be successful and make a lot of money. He possessed the optimistic feeling widespread at the time that anything could be accomplished with drive and determination. He believed that in America rewards belonged to those who accomplished great things, and that there was nothing wrong with getting rich. But he also believed that the work of people like himself was good for all Americans, by providing jobs and raising the standard of living for everyone. George Westinghouse was an idealist who wanted to do good things for his country, but he was also a hardheaded businessman who wanted to do well for himself in the process.

As should be clear, technological advances were racing forward at an astonishing speed in the years after the Civil War: The Bessemer process for making steel in 1856, the first oil well in 1859, the air brake in 1868, the electric streetcar in 1874, the dynamo for producing electric power in 1875, the telephone in 1876, the phonograph in 1878, the incandescent bulb in 1879, the electric welding machine in 1886, the automobile in the 1890s, the airplane in 1903. Any one of these inventions would have had dramatic effects on American life; all of them coming along in a rush as they did, simply turned American society upside down. By 1900 we were no longer a nation of farmers as we had been a mere thirty years before; we were a great industrial nation built around huge, sprawling, tumultuous cities.

CHAPTER II

The Coming of the Railroad

Sprawling as the nation was, industrial development would have gotten no place without the parallel development of the railroad. Invented in England and first established there in the 1820s, steam locomotive engines (as distinguished from the stationary engine used in factories) came quickly to America, and were sooner and more widely applied to transportation on water and railroads than in factories.

It is necessary to step back to the preindustrial early nineteenth century to trace the history of our nation's railroads. The first railroad lines in America were built in the 1820s; in 1825 John Stevens had produced the first American-built railway steam engine. Previously, most American transportation was by water. Roads were rough, hardly more than mere paths through the forests in some places. It was far easier to carry both freight and people by boat up and down rivers, along the ocean coasts, and through the huge canal system dug out in the 1820s and 1830s. After a period of experimentation and development, railroad trains came to have great advantages over sail or steamboats. Locomotives could travel much faster than riverboats and canal barges, and were not subject to changes in wind and tides; railroad lines did not

The Englishman James Watt shown in his laboratory, studying improvements for his steam engine. The steam engine dramatically changed people's lives in Europe and the United States.

flood in the spring and freeze in the winter, as northern rivers and canals did.

The spread of railroad lines through the American countryside was rapid. In 1830 there were only 546 miles of rails in New York State; none in Virginia; and only 1,277 in the nation as a whole. By 1860, just before the Civil War, New York had 2,682 miles of track, Virginia 1,731, and the country altogether 30,636. By the end of the war, in the late 1860s, the railroads had pushed across the Mississippi River and were rapidly spreading over the Great Plains toward the Rockies, and would link the coasts by 1869.

The DeWitt Clinton, *riding the first New York State railroad, of 1831, could travel at the "frightful speed" of fifteen miles an hour, slow by present standards, but then much faster than horses pulling a heavy load could move. The railroad "cars" were modeled on the ordinary carriages usually drawn by horses.*

This railroad system was badly organized, indeed chaotic. It had been constructed piecemeal by investors looking to make profits from putting up a line from one city to the next. In most nations the railroad system was built and run by the government, and great, longterm plans were developed before lines were constructed. But the United States economy is based on the idea of private free enterprise where development is left up to individuals seeking a profit for themselves. Thus nobody in government or outside of it had sat down and worked out a coherent long-range plan. Many of the lines were quite small. They used several track widths, or "gauges," which meant that frequently freight going through a city had to be unloaded from cars using one gauge and reloaded into cars with another one.

This huge railroad boom could not have been financed solely by investors. Even while they promoted free-enterprise ideas, private developers called for government help. As the railroads began to link towns and cities together, officials in many places panicked lest they be left out of the system. Business, they feared, would flow along railroad lines, as indeed it did. Cities, counties, states, and even small towns began subsidizing railroad companies, giving them land for track and stations, tax breaks, and often outright cash payments.

The Federal government, too, strongly favored building a great national railway system. After the Mexican War of the 1840s and the California gold rush of 1849, the West was opened up to settlement by Americans. Congress was very keen on seeing this land filled with farmers, miners, lumbermen, and other productive settlers. It wanted transcontinental railways built to carry people and goods quickly and safely across the deserts and prairies. However, there was a problem. The railroad lines would have to be built *before* there were any large numbers of customers out in the West to use them. The farmers, settlers, and cattle ranchers would come only after the lines were built.

Congress thus began making huge grants of land to the railroad companies to encourage them to invest. This land was not limited to what was needed for the laying of track and the putting up of stations. The land grants were many miles wide along the planned routes. This land would become very valuable once the railroad tracks were laid; the railroad companies could sell it at huge profits—profits they could use to build yet more miles of railway. During the great railroad boom from the 1850s to the 1880s, American cities, states, and the national government gave away tens of millions of acres of public land to the railroads—almost 50 million acres from the states, 130 million acres from the Federal government—an amount of land bigger than the present state of Texas.

By 1840, only a few years later, passenger cars had been modernized, and hundreds of miles of railroad track already crisscrossed the eastern part of the nation.

But the U.S. government did not give the railroads only land. It also loaned them tens of millions of dollars. Needless to say, with so much money being thrown around by local, state, and national governments, cheating was inevitable. For one thing, some of the railroad promoters collected money from cities to build railroad lines, and then never bothered to lay any rails. In other cases the lines were built, but construction was shoddy and the materials used were cheap; cities sometimes found that after having paid to have a line built, they had to pay again to put the line in good working order.

One of the most widely used devices for cheating governments was for the people who owned the railroad companies to form their own construction companies. They would then hire themselves to build railroad lines, paid for by government loans and subsidies, in most cases vastly overcharging for the work.

Laying track across the vast spaces of the western plains and over the mountains was an enormous job, but was accomplished in a decade. The railroad companies needed huge subsidies from the U.S. government, which they often misused. Note the little town of about two dozen houses growing up along the railroad tracks. The railroads were given an immense amount of land along the lines, which they sold at high profits to speculators.

But, however scandal ridden and economically unsound, a huge system was brought into being. Particularly after the Civil War broke out there was pressure to standardize the track gauge: After many negotiations, the railroad companies settled on a standard track width of 4'8½". Schedules, too, were coordinated. This had one important side effect. Up until 1883, towns, cities, and states used whatever time system they wanted. There were some fifty-four different times at use in the United States, creating much confusion in train schedules. In 1883 the railroads finally agreed on the time zones used in the United States today: Eastern, Central, Rocky Mountain, and Pacific time.

As the practical problems were solved, the railroads became not merely important but essential to the lives of millions of Americans. Farmers settled on the western lands along the lines, counting on the railroads to ship their wheat, corn, and cattle to city markets back East. Farmers everywhere grew dependent on the rails. Coal mine operators, copper and iron ore miners, and smelters of iron and steel could hardly stay in business without the railroads to carry their large-scale produce around the country. Inevitably, the railroads took advantage of this dependency when they could.

And often they could. We remember that initially railroads were built to tie one city to another one nearby. Only later were these small lines linked together in larger systems. Very often the lines from city to city were monopolies—that is to say, there was only one line traveling between these particular two cities. Either you shipped your wheat, steel, and cloth on that line, or you didn't ship it at all. (In some cases riverboats and canal barges provided an alternative—often seasonal; but in many instances, particularly on the Western plains, there was no alternative to the local railroad.)

Not surprisingly, whenever a railroad had a monopoly, it would set shipping rates as high as possible. According to one report, an Ohio farmer who shipped his corn to Massachusetts was paid 68¢ a bushel; freight charges were 67¢ a bushel. It was calculated that Minnesota wheat growers were paid in one year $8 million for their grain, but the railroads got $12 million for shipping it.

Making matters worse, railroads built their own grain elevators— huge silolike warehouses—for storing wheat at the depots. If farmers wanted their grain shipped, they had to use the railroads' elevators, and pay whatever the railroads charged for the service. Even if the farmer did not actually need to use the elevator, he was often charged for the storage anyway.

This unprincipled gouging by the railroads often inevitably caused an uproar. Farmers began to revolt and by the 1870s were badgering their state legislatures to do something about the situation. Soon they were joined by small businessmen in the country towns. The railroads responded by bribing legislators, judges, and town officials. Passes on the railroads showered down on government officials like "snow in a winter storm," as somebody said. Legislators were given stock in the railroads, often outright cash. Nonetheless, the unfair practices of the railroad monopolies were so obvious that they could not be covered over, and various laws were passed to curb the worst of the abuses. Among other things, railroads were required to post official rates, so that shippers could compare prices, to see if the rates were reasonable.

But in the fight between the railroads and the shippers, the railroads had a lot of advantages. For one thing, as we shall see in more detail later, there has always been a strong feeling that governments ought not to interfere in private business, even when the business in question, like the railroads, has great national importance. Courts, legislators, and congressmen were uneasy about interfering with business decisions and forcing the railroads to charge reasonable prices and otherwise deal fairly with farmers and other shippers.

As a consequence, the railroad owners and managers continued to get away with many shady practices. Our private free-enterprise system depends on competition among many companies to keep prices down and quality up. But railroad managers often formed pools among themselves, secretly setting high rates. Sometimes they would cut rates to powerful large-scale shippers, like big steel or oil companies. In other instances railroads had business links with other shippers and industrialists: The Reading Railroad in Pennsylvania, for instance, was sole owner of the Reading Coal and Iron Company, and could charge its own company low shipping rates while charging other coal and iron companies much higher rates.

All of these practices led to some very strange situations. At one point Reading's stove coal, used in homes for cooking and heating, was priced at $4.80 a ton in downtown Philadelphia, but $3.75 in Port Richmond, a part of the same city. In another case a merchant from Wilkes-Barre, Pennsylvania, discovered that it cost more to ship a load of potatoes from Rochester to Wilkes-Barre than to Philadelphia, farther down the line. He shipped his potatoes to Philadelphia at the lower price, but had them unloaded when the train stopped at Wilkes-Barre. The railroad managers found out what he had done, and sent him a bill for not carrying the potatoes on to Philadelphia.

Despite all these abuses, the development of the railroad industry, linking American cities and towns in a cheap transportation system, provided a crucial base for the creation of the industrial machine. Without the railroads it would have been difficult, if not impossible, for industries like oil, steel, copper, cattle, and lumber to operate. These industries had to bring into factories huge amounts of raw material—iron ore, coal, unrefined oil, lumber—and to ship out equally huge amounts of finished goods—steel, fuel oil, rails. The railroads provided a cheap and efficient way to transport these goods.

But as should be clear, the railroad system was built haphazardly, piecemeal, by promoters and investors looking for quick profits more than out of a desire to give the nation good transportation. Abuses were rampant. Lying, cheating, bribery, and chicanery were everywhere. Regrettably, this pattern was to be followed by other industries as they rose up in America in the decades after the Civil War. And finally, as we shall see, the Federal government would have to step in to try to stop the worst abuses.

CHAPTER III

The Rise of the
Large Corporation

Human societies have always found ways of organizing themselves. People form clusters around certain activities. After they have become established in a set of fixed relationships, this collection of people—usually with common objectives, rules, and buildings—can be referred to as an *institution*. One of the most important of all institutions in the United States—and indeed in most industrial nations—is the business corporation. (There are other types of corporations, such as charities and cities and towns.) The names of many of these business corporations are household words: Ford, Microsoft, Coca-Cola, American Airlines, NBC—anyone could write out a long list. Taken together, these corporations make up what is sometimes called "big business." These corporations have immense power. The largest 500 of them account for 75 percent of all American manufacturing profits. They employ a great portion of all American workers and produce more than half of American goods. Most Americans are deeply involved with these huge corporations, working in their shops and offices, getting to and from those jobs in their cars, trains, and buses, spending their spare time using their products around the home.

The big corporations are so much with us today that we often forget how large a role they play in our lives, not only supplying us with services and products we need but occupying our working hours, giving us our pay, and more indirectly, influencing our governments. These trade names are utterly familiar to Americans.

And they are huge. Some of these corporations, like General Electric and General Motors, are international giants, with tens of thousands of employees, doing business all around the world, with branches in cities as different as Bangkok, Rome, and Tel Aviv. Some corporations take in more money each year than the entire economies of many small countries.

The institution of the large corporation first arose in the United States in the period we are studying, roughly the years between the end of the

Civil War in 1865 and 1900. Corporations, or similar arrangements, had existed before. The English adventurers who financed many of the early settlements in America were often formed into corporations. These early corporations were partly private, partly governmental. They were owned by private investors out for profits, but they were chartered by English kings and queens for the good of the English nation and were given operating rules by government.

The modern American corporation began to develop in the early 1800s when many *states* worked out rules for chartering them. The idea was to encourage people to start businesses that would do something for the public good. Thus, a state might charter a private corporation to build a toll bridge over a river. The investors would make money from the tolls, and the public would be able to cross the river by bridge instead of on a ferry. We need to keep this idea in mind, that corporations were originally set up in order to *serve the public* by encouraging people to invest in various kinds of socially useful projects.

In order to give that encouragement, governments began to grant corporations *limited liability*. What that means is that if the corporation gets into financial trouble, the corporation, not the investors, is responsible for its debts. If an unincorporated company owned by an individual or some group of partners fails, then the company's creditors can take the private property—cars, houses, etc.—from all the individual owners. But, if a corporation fails, the investors lose only the money they invested. They do not have to put up further money to make good on the debts of the corporation. It is easy to see how this encourages investment, for a wealthy man might be willing to gamble a small part of his money when he knows that the rest of his money will be protected. (And, realistically, it is only wealthy people who have the money to invest in projects, like bridges, canals, and textile factories, that the state and Federal governments believe will be for the general good.)

The corporation has another advantage. Usually, each investor buys so many "shares" in a project—each of ten investors might take 1,000 shares. If an investor suddenly needs the money for something else, he can usually sell some or all of his shares to another investor. This system provides investors with *liquidity*—that is, their money can flow easily in and out of various investments as prospects for one or another of them change. And, of course, the corporation is *immortal*—that is, it lives on and on no matter how many—or even if all—of its stockholders die.

The institution of the corporation proved to be crucially important in building the railroad system. This was especially true of the transcontinental railroads stretching out into the unsettled Great Plains, which would not pay off until farms had been established and towns built along them. Many of these early railroad corporations did run into trouble, through mismanagement, ill luck, and corrupt practices. Without the limited liability that incorporation provided, later investors—and, of course, these huge projects needed thousands of them—would have been scared off by early railway failures, and the settling of the West would have gone far slower.

Another very important part of the philosophy behind the corporations was that they were artificial *persons* (though, as we have seen, immortal ones). This idea had been around for awhile, and in a couple of important rulings, the Supreme Court made it official. The consequences of the rulings were major, and have a great deal to do with how our society works today. If a corporation is a person, it must be entitled to all the rights that human beings have under the U.S. Constitution. For the corporations, the most important of these rights was spelled out in the Fourteenth Amendment, which says, "Nor shall any state deprive any person of life, liberty, or property, without due process of law." The Fourteenth Amendment had been put into the Constitution after the Civil War to keep Southerners from pressing the recently freed slaves back into serfdom; it had nothing to do with the corporations. But in 1872 the Supreme Court applied it to corporations. It said, in effect, if a state government passed laws setting minimum wages, limiting hours of work, or requiring safe and healthy working conditions for workers, it would deprive the corporation of its property—that is to say, money lost from profits by these regulations.

Treating corporations as "persons" was not only part of the American legal tradition but it also fit in with the idea that business would be more efficiently run—and thus better for everyone—if it were left alone by government. The Supreme Court never gave any reason for saying that corporations were to be considered people. The Court of that time believed that the large corporations like the railway lines were bringing great prosperity to the nation, and ought not to be interfered with. Many people agreed.

This belief was based on the idea of private free-enterprise capitalism regulated by competition. According to this theory, anyone should be allowed to start any business he wants to—so long as it does no damage to the health or morals of the people. When somebody starts to make a lot of money out of an industry like railroads, oil, or electric lights, other people will jump in and invest capital in similar businesses. Soon a number of companies will be competing for customers either by charging less for the same product, improving the product, or both.

Thus, competition will force prices down and constantly bring new and improved products. In this theory, competition, the heart of the free-enterprise system, will automatically work for the good of everybody. Governments should therefore leave the system alone to run itself.

As usual, theory and practice soon proved to be not quite the same thing. Almost from the moment that the large corporations began to grow in post–Civil War years, the people who ran them began trying to get around the "natural law" of competition. Businessmen could see clearly enough that while competition might be good for the nation as a whole, it was not usually very good for their own businesses. Businessmen, of course, wanted to charge the highest prices they thought

In the theory of capitalism, competition is supposed to keep prices down and improve products. At left, an array of competing breakfast foods in a supermarket. Below, two pastry shops side-by-side compete for customers.

they could get away with and still attract customers; competition often forced prices down to the point that nobody in a given industry was able to make much money. One manufacturer of envelopes said bluntly, "Competition is industrial war . . . Unrestricted competition, carried to its logical conclusion, means death to some of the combatants and injury for all."

So the corporations began looking for ways around competition. One scheme was called a "pool." The details of the pools could be complicated, but the basic idea was simple enough: A group of supposedly competitive businessmen in a certain industry would quietly agree to charge the same price for the same product or agree not to sell their product or service in each other's territories.

There was not yet any specific law against these pools, but they were seen as unethical. The pools forced people to pay higher prices than they would have otherwise. They also pushed prices up for businessmen who needed the goods and services produced by the pools. For example, steel and coal operators were sometimes forced by the railroad pools to pay more for transportation than they felt they should. Businessmen, thus, often opposed pools, at least those they themselves were not part of. Since they violated Anglo-American traditional business ethics, pool agreements could not be enforced in court. And sooner or later some pool members would begin to cheat on the others in the pool, quietly offering their customers prices lower than the pool prices. In most cases the pools soon fell apart in cheating and bickering.

Soon another method for getting around competition was worked out. Any activity that was making profits, especially big profits, was soon filled with dozens, or even hundreds, of firms. This happened in the oil business. Within weeks after Edwin Drake brought in the first oil well, drilling machinery was rising all over the landscape. The little town of Pithole, Pennsylvania, grew from 100 people to 14,000 in nine months in 1865. (It shrunk almost as fast when the neighboring area was pumped out.) All of these hundreds of independent oil companies, most of them small, competed to drive the price of oil down.

To get rid of the competition, a system of "trusts" was worked out by the staff of the oil tycoon John D. Rockefeller. Rockefeller's idea was to buy up as many of the competing oil companies as he could, in order to cut down on the competition. It was illegal for one corporation to own stock in another one, so trusts were set up. These trusts would not themselves create anything—produce oil or refine it. They would simply own the stock of real, producing companies. Rockefeller's trust was the Standard Oil Company, and in time it gave him control of half of the American oil industry, which permitted him to control the price of oil. People in other industries quickly saw the usefulness of trusts, and formed their own. Through the last years of the 1890s and the early years of the 1900s, hundreds of companies were consolidated into trusts by powerful corporate magnates like J. P. Morgan, who in 1901 pulled together some 200 steel companies to form U.S. Steel, which soon owned 1,000 miles of railroads, 112 blast furnaces, and 78 ore boats. U.S. Steel controlled 60 percent of American steel production and employed 170,000 workers.

The same was happening in other industries. General Electric and Westinghouse in

John Pierpont Morgan was one of the most powerful of the money lords who ruled much of the American economy in the late 1800s. As a banker, he supplied a lot of the capital needed to form the great trusts that consolidated smaller corporations under one head, such as U.S. Steel, which Morgan helped to put together.

electrical equipment, International Harvester in farm equipment, U.S. Rubber, American Brass, and many, many others were formed by consolidating a lot of corporations in one industry into one great trust.

These consolidations brought together many or most of the manufacturers of a certain product: bicycles, paint, glass, etc. These are called *horizontal* monopolies. (To be considered a monopoly, a business does not have to control *all* the production of a certain item or service, but just enough to effectively set the price for all.)

Another form of market control took place through the *vertical* monopoly. Vertical organization occurs when one corporation owns all the necessary elements of its product. The Armour and Swift meat-packing companies are examples of this. They owned not only their own slaughterhouses but also their own farms, stockyards, cattle, and refrigerated railway cars, and processing and packaging plants. Vertical organization allowed not only bulk purchase and transportation but also eliminated profit-taking by middlemen at each stage of production.

These consolidations did have many advantages. For one thing, they were *economies of scale*: if you make a lot of something, you can sometimes make it cheaper than if you only make a few. For example, one team of accountants could keep books on millions of dollars as easily as thousands, one advertising writer could write the ad for a product that sold millions as easily as for one that sold thousands. For another, these large corporations made available to Americans vast quantities of goods few could have afforded before, or, indeed, goods that hadn't even existed before. They also provided a lot of jobs. Most of them, as we shall shortly see, were hard jobs with long hours and low pay, the so-called "blue collar," or production, jobs. But the large corporations also needed a lot of "white collar" office workers—filing clerks, salesmen, secretaries, department managers, accountants, lawyers, and many more. Thus the corporations in this post–Civil War period created a whole middle class of white-collar workers that had not really existed in the United

States before, at least not in a large way. These people, usually better educated, had easier jobs and in many cases much better pay and higher status than the workers on the shop floor. They were able to afford comfortably sized apartments, even houses. They could dress well, own nice furnishings for their homes, give dinner parties, and make holiday trips and excursions to the seashore or the mountains.

Perhaps more important, they believed that they could advance in their jobs, perhaps to positions of real authority and high income. Their children, too, did not have to go to work at early ages, but could stay in school, even go to college (only about one of a hundred Americans attended college at the turn of the century) and themselves go into business or the professions.

This new middle class of white-collar workers had mainly come off the farms in the broad movement to the city from the farms we have seen. But very quickly they, or their children and grandchildren, developed a culture that differed from the older culture of the farmlands, or the various cultures being brought in by immigrants. For these white-collar workers, hard work, promptness, and taking an interest in the job would pay off in a way it would not for manual laborers. (Laboring people certainly worked hard enough; but for them hard work and taking an interest in the job did not often pay off in promotions and pay raises.) It also became important for this middle class to have good manners, speak good English, dress neatly according to the new styles, generally behave in a polite way. This middle-class culture became a kind of model, a norm for Americans. And several decades later, when blue-collar workers began to earn decent salaries, they, too, adopted this style, with its good manners, nicely furnished homes, and attractive clothes. This middle class, with its culture, was one of the most important changes the new industrial system brought to America.

The middle class was one of the major beneficiaries of the rising prosperity in America. But those who benefited most were a tiny minority of

By the end of the 1800s there had arisen in the United States a new middle class of so-called white-collar workers, employed mainly by the large corporations as managers, clerks, salesmen, and more. This new middle class was developing a comfortable lifestyle, exemplified by this pleasant suburban community situated in Richmond Hill, on the fringes of New York City.

investors, promoters, entrepreneurs, and such who rose to the top of the system, gaining great power and enormous wealth, greater in terms of that time than all except the largest fortunes being amassed today. These people have been called "robber barons" by some historians, and there is no doubt that many of them got their wealth and power by unscrupulous, even illegal methods, like bribery, the pools, riding roughshod over weaker competitors, and at their worst, actually bringing in armed men to fight, and even kill, workers who struck for higher wages.

It has long been a belief in America that many men rose from poverty to great wealth through hard work, self-sacrifice, and perhaps a little luck. A writer of post–Civil War years named Horatio Alger wrote many very popular rags-to-riches tales of poor but honest boys who made successes of themselves, and the term "Horatio Alger myth" has clung to such stories. But, as careful studies have shown, most of the men who gained wealth and power had been born pretty far up the ladder, into families of businessmen and professionals. They usually were better educated than most, and often had access to at least a little money to get them started, and almost always had connections in business. As unlikely as a rise from rags to riches was, however, millions of young men read Horatio Alger's books—he wrote about two hundred of them—and were inspired to work hard, save their money, and look for the main chance. Very few of them ever got rich, but they usually were able to provide comfortable lives for their families, and often rose a notch or two on the social scale.

Perhaps a near approximation of the rise to fabulous wealth is shown in the life of John D. Rockefeller, who was born in 1839 and became, according to one historian, "the most reviled and in many respects the greatest of American moguls." Rockefeller's father was a flamboyant and unscrupulous roving seller of fake medicines, one of many of that time. Sometimes he made money, sometimes not, but young John was able to get some education, and at eighteen borrowed $1,000 from his father to start his own business. It prospered. Meanwhile, Edwin Drake had drilled his oil well and the oil boom was on. Rockefeller looked into it, and decided that the money was to be made not in the chaotic drilling business but in refining crude oil into other products, mainly kerosene for lamps and stoves. He organized various partnerships, and began shipping by rail large quantities of oil into his refineries in Cleveland, Ohio, and then shipping out the kerosene.

Rockefeller then decided he must control all oil refined in the United States, and he set about creating a monopoly. To do this he went to the railroad company servicing the Cleveland area and demanded a secret rebate of freight charges. That is, the railroad line would bill Rockefeller's company the regular rate, but then "kick back" a portion

The early oil drills were exceedingly primitive compared with modern ones. This is one of Drake's early ones, in western Pennsylvania. It was soon surrounded by hundreds of others like it.

of the fees. In effect, Rockefeller would pay lower shipping rates and could thus sell his oil cheaper than his competition could.

Now, through persuasion, threats of price warfare, and other methods, he got other competitors to come into his rapidly growing Standard Oil Company. In one case he secretly set up a company called Acme Oil Company, which supposedly was an independent company determined to battle the "octopus" of Standard Oil. Acme persuaded some twenty independent refiners who wanted to battle Rockefeller to join up with it. Once they had signed, they discovered that Acme was under the control of Standard Oil. They had been duped.

Through methods such as these, by 1878 John D. Rockefeller, thirty-nine years old, controlled 95 percent of the refineries and pipelines in the

The name of John D. Rockefeller is synonymous with great wealth—the phrase "rich as Rockefeller" turns up in songs. A devout, churchgoing man, he was nonetheless ruthless in business, leaving in his path, as one critic said, "ruined men and abandoned plants."

United States. He could set prices almost as he liked. And by the 1880s Rockefeller was "supreme" in the business of refining oil. According to one historian, the upward path trodden by Rockefeller was "strewn with ruined men and abandoned plants." The path would continue upward, to enormous wealth and power. Rockefeller's descendants remain enormously wealthy, have become governors, congressmen, even a vice president of the United States.

The story of John D. Rockefeller and Standard Oil was repeated by other robber barons: Cornelius Vanderbilt and Jay Gould in railroads, J. P. Morgan in finance, Andrew Carnegie in steel. These people gained their wealth mainly by creating monopolies, or something close to them. In doing so they often trampled on competitors, bribed government officials, and overcharged the public when they could. Some of them, in their private lives, could appear to be decent human beings: Rockefeller was a devout churchgoer, and lived relatively modestly, considering the fact that he was one of the richest people in the world. Andrew Carnegie

Corporations, according to capitalist theory, were supposed to operate for the public benefit, but often they did not. Cornelius Vanderbilt, another of the "robber barons," expressed the attitude of many such men when he said, "The public be damned."

eventually gave away the bulk of his huge fortune, building libraries everywhere in the United States, and financing other buildings, like New York's Carnegie Hall.

Furthermore, the corporations helped to bring great material wealth to the nation, from which the new middle class, especially, benefited. Also benefiting were lower-middle class and laboring families who could now buy household items that were too expensive in the preindustrial era—or, indeed, hadn't existed at all. The activity of the great industrialists created thousands of new kinds of jobs and new products at prices that most Americans could afford and of a quality more often than not better than the old handmade. The great industrial corporations also provided millions of jobs for the millions of impoverished, unskilled immigrants pouring into America's fast-growing cities. (For that story see the volume in "The Drama of American History" called *A Century of Immigration*.)

But the corporations—or the men who ran them—also brought a change of attitude to America, which was not always a blessing. As we have seen, the corporations originally were given certain advantages, like limited liability and liquidity, because they were supposed to be doing things that were for the public good. But by the time Rockefeller, Carnegie, and Vanderbilt were trying to create their monopolies in oil, steel, and railroads, men running the corporations had abandoned the idea that they ought to be working for the public good. Indeed one of them, Cornelius Vanderbilt, when once asked about it, said flatly, "The public be damned." To these people, the first job of the corporations was to make profits for the owners, that is, those who held stock in them. The interests of others, like the employees, the suppliers, the customers, and the nation as a whole, came second, or in many cases not at all.

In any case, for better or worse, by 1900 the great corporations had come to stay. But any sweeping change like this produces problems: The new industrial system brought not prosperity, but troubles and woe to millions of Americans who did not share in the wealth.

CHAPTER IV

The Problems
with Industrialization

The people building the mighty industrial system, like Carnegie, Vanderbilt, and Rockefeller, needed raw materials like iron ore and coal. They also needed a great deal of shipping to bring the raw materials of their factories and finished product to the markets all over the United States. But what they needed most of all was *labor*, provided by the millions of Americans who worked in the factories, the mines, on railroads, and ships. Just as it was in their interest to drive shipping prices down through devices like rebates, and get their raw material as cheaply as possible through monopoly control and other arrangements, so it was important to them to keep the price of labor as low as possible.

There was a difference, however: Raw materials and railroad cars did not have human feelings, and labor did. Many industrialists, however, did not make this distinction. Their duty was to making profits, and if that meant keeping wages down, that was the way things were, even when many a worker had trouble buying food and shelter for his family on his wages. Said Andrew Carnegie, "The worker has no more to do with setting his wages than does a piece of coal with setting its price."

Let us see how such people, the industrial workers (as opposed to those on farms) who made up 40 percent of the American population, actually lived. Most of them worked an average of about ten hours a day, six days a week, although there were lucky ones who had achieved the eight-hour day, and some unlucky ones who worked twelve hours a day. (There was no such thing as "the weekend" we know today. Everybody, including the bosses, worked on Saturday.)

Many of these jobs were physically exhausting. Some people might have relatively easy, if boring, tasks at sewing machines or drill presses, but most were carrying bricks up ladders, digging coal with picks and shovels, or loading freight cars. One brass worker in Waterbury, Connecticut, recalled work in the casting shop where the men used tongs to handle red-hot bars of metal ten hours a day and inhaled metal-oxide fumes. It was "just like the coal-mines where you got the black lung. For

Lacking the power tools and mechanical hoists we take for granted today, much labor was simple drudgery. This hod carrier spent ten or twelve hours a day carrying bricks up ladders in the "hod" he has over his shoulder. This photograph was taken by Jacob Riis, who specialized in recording the lives of working people.

awhile there, almost every week somebody would drop dead of a heart attack." In that mill in one year there were 16,000 accidents, 11,287 casualties, and 60,000 surgical dressings given to the workers. But mostly the work in industrial plants was just plain boring: a certain hand motion repeated over and over hundreds, even thousands, of times a day.

This closely confined, regimented labor contrasted sharply with the work in the early-nineteenth-century craft shops where skilled artisans constructed saddles, silver tea sets, blown-glass bottles, and the like, performing all the processes, working at his own pace, and taking tea breaks pretty much when he felt like it. The industrial plants of the late nineteenth century were more like the textile mills of the 1840s and 1850s, but far more dangerous and unhealthy.

For this hard work and long hours ordinary workers earned about $400 a year in 1900, worth about $12,000 a year at the end of the twentieth century. It was calculated at the time that a family of four needed about $800 a year just to scrape along. This meant that in most working families the children had to go to work as soon as they could. Even children as young as six often worked at simple jobs, like picking out good coal from ashes, in order to earn a few badly needed pennies. At fourteen—in some states younger—children were considered to be capable of doing the work of adults and could legally get jobs. As a result, few of the children of workers could get the schooling that might have lifted them out of lives of poverty and drudgery.

But workers could not always count on earning even this rock-bottom income. During the decades we are studying there were several serious economic crises, one about every ten years: deep depressions that affected farmers as well as industrial employees, white- and blue-collar, devastated families' incomes for five years beginning in 1873 and again from 1893 to 1897. Massive unemployment hit industrial workers at such times and thousands were laid off for weeks or even months. Workers might also be laid off even during good times when new machinery was being installed, because of seasonal fluctuation in demand for fur coats and summer cottons, even because of the weather: When the canals froze over, bargemen would lose work, and so might workers dependent on raw materials brought in by barge. Before the 1930s there was no such thing as unemployment insurance: If you were out of work you earned no money except what you could scrape up doing odd jobs. In Massachusetts, at the turn of the century, 30 percent of all workers lost many days of work every year. Only a quarter of railroad men worked a full year; 60 percent were out of work fully half the time.

Earning so little, it is inevitable that this 40 percent of Americans lived very mean, even desperate lives. Half their incomes went for food, and a quarter for rent, leaving them about 50¢ to 75¢ a day for clothes, carfare, a newspaper and recreation, which meant that for most of them recreation amounted to a pipeful of tobacco, an occasional glass of beer, a walk in the park.

They lived, most of them, in two- or three-room apartments in tenement buildings that were being hastily built in the rapidly growing cities. Children slept two or three to a bed and adults often shared beds as well. Many of these tenements did not have running water: It had to be carried in buckets up as many as six flights of stairs. (These tenements did not have elevators.) The apartments were heated by kerosene or coal stoves, and the fuel also had to be carried up all those stairs. There was never any privacy in these apartments, no place where a family member could get off by himself to read or study.

Young women were expected to work until they got married. They were paid only about half of what men earned, and had to turn most or all of their wages over to their families, who could not manage without the extra money.

The situation was even worse for African-Americans. Black men almost always got only the hardest, lowest-paid jobs. This meant that black women almost certainly had to work to contribute to the family income, which in turn meant that children were cared for by neighbors or relatives, or were not supervised at all.

On top of it, many jobs in the new industrial system were dangerous, some of them extremely so. (Admittedly, farm jobs could also be dangerous.) According to one historian, the United States in the late 1800s had

Another photograph from the Jacob Riis collection, showing a typical tenement apartment in a New York City slum. The seven members of this family shared three beds—the crib, the narrow bed in the foreground, and the larger bed in the room at back. The stove in the left front served both for heat and cooking. Coal for it had to be carried up several flights of stairs in buckets. Millions of Americans, especially immigrants, lived in apartments like this well into the twentieth century.

A necktie workroom in a tenement. Women were favored for jobs like this, because they could be paid less than men. These tenements were firetraps: In the famous Triangle Shirtwaist factory fire of 1911, 146 people, mostly young women, burned to death or died jumping from windows when they could not escape the burning building.

one of the highest industrial accident rates in the Western industrial world. In the two decades from 1880 to 1900, 35,000 workers were killed each year on the job, and 536,000 were injured, many of them permanently crippled. There was no medical insurance, no workmen's compensation to help those who were crippled in an accident and could no longer work. Such people either begged, or depended on their families to support them.

And these conditions were *average*: Millions of agricultural workers were even worse off, like Southern sharecroppers living in cabins, or migratory harvesters in California who lived in tents or filthy barracks, sharing outdoor toilets with twenty or thirty people. The effects of poverty could be seen in the children. "Their faces. . . are peculiarly aged in expression, and their eyes gleam with premature knowledge, which is the result of a daily struggle, not for life, but existence" wrote an observer of children in a Pittsburgh steel mine.

There was, however, an elite of workers who were substantially better off. These were people in skilled trades that required years of training, like the engineers who drove the railroad trains, engravers who made the copper plates from which newspaper and magazine pictures were printed, and machinists who cut metal parts for precision instruments. Highly trained skilled workers like these could not be easily replaced. As a consequence they could demand higher wages. Some of them earned as much as $900 a year, as much as white-collar workers in offices made. These "aristocrats of labor," as they have been called, often owned their own homes, could go out to the variety shows popular at the time, could keep their children out of the workplace so they could get some education, and perhaps move into white-collar jobs and the middle class.

But the "aristocrats of labor" made up around 15 percent of the industrial laboring population. The other 85 percent lived in tenements, ate the cheapest possible food, and scraped desperately from day to day.

It must be remembered that around 20 percent of these working people were immigrants, who had been born in Europe, China, and elsewhere; a great many others were the American-born children of immigrants. By the end of the period we are studying, half of the inhabitants of some big cities like New York were the foreign-born and their children. (The story of immigrants in America is told in detail in the volume in this series entitled *A Century of Immigration*.)

Clearly, by 1900 the United States had become a nation divided into

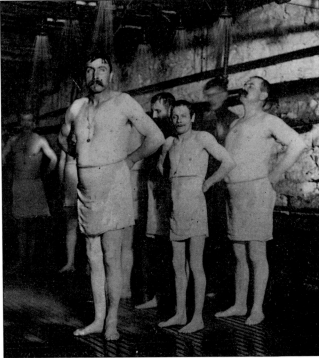

Above: If conditions for immigrants were bad, they were worse for African-Americans. These sharecroppers in the backwoods of Georgia lived in a log cabin, and ate mainly pork and cornbread.

Left: Another picture by Jacob Riis. Some workers did not even have their own apartments, but lived in lodging provided by the city. They were required to take showers in this public bath.

"the haves and the have nots." As early as 1870, when the industrial system was still cranking up, the richest 1 percent of Americans held over a quarter of the wealth, while the poorest *half* owned only 1 percent of the wealth. By 1890 the top 1 percent owned half of the wealth, the bottom 44 percent just over 1 percent. The top 12 percent had 86 percent of the wealth, the other 88 percent of Americans had 14 percent of the wealth.

How could a nation that takes pride in being fair let such a huge discrepancy between the very rich and everybody else come about? It is a truism that human beings can generally find rationalizations for doing things they really want to do. The people at the top wanted their wealth, regardless of how working people suffered, and they found justification in the theories of an English philosopher named Herbert Spencer. One of Spencer's main ideas was the "law of equal freedom." This said that everybody ought to be able to do anything they wanted so long as it did not hurt someone else.

A second part of Spencer's theory he called the "law of cause and consequence": Every individual was responsible for everything that happened to them. Spencer made no allowance for luck, advantages of coming from a wealthy family, etc.

Inevitably, some people will succeed and others will fail, but this is as it should be: the "fittest" will reap the rewards, those less fit will fall by the wayside. (Spencer later supported his theory with evidence for Charles Darwin's theory of evolution, so Spencer's philosophy is sometimes called Social Darwinism. But it really has little, if anything, to do with Darwin's work.) Under this theory the "less fit" will die off, the "most fit" will rise, and society will gradually improve.

But according to Spencer, the system will only work if governments do not interfere, to help or hinder anyone. Competition must operate unimpeded. The sick and stupid must fall by the wayside along with the lazy and immoral. The final conclusion was that governments should do nothing except to provide for defense against foreign nations, and admin-

Herbert Spencer was an English philosopher who worked out a theory that justified the right of some people to amass great wealth, while others lived in tiny tenements and hovels, and worked at grinding jobs. Spencer's theories were popular with better-off Americans and were referred to by courts in making decisions favorable to industrial leaders. This caricature gives the artist's idea of the philosopher.

ister justice to prevent the competitors from using violence against each other. Government, declared Spencer, should consist of nothing more than a policeman and a judge. Spencer did not believe that governments ought to help the poor, the aged, or the ill, for that was interfering with the system. He did not even believe that governments ought to mint coins or provide schools—people should see about educating their children themselves.

Not surprisingly, Herbert Spencer's ideas appealed strongly to the wealthy businessmen atop the industrial system. They liked Spencer's idea that since they had proved themselves the fittest by having come out on top, they were therefore entitled to their wealth. The middle class also welcomed Spencer's ideas, for they, too, could believe they had proved themselves more fit than others, and did not have to feel guilty about those less well off. And, inspired by Horatio Alger as we have seen, they hoped that they, too, would someday be among the wealthy few. Further, Spencer's theories showed why it was wrong for governments to try to control the corporations to benefit workers and customers: These people were best fitted to labor and should be allowed to remain at their "natural" level and leave money in the hands of those who had proven themselves most fit to manage it.

There were similar theories going around. Andrew Carnegie put forth the idea, which he had not invented, that anyone who was smart, ambitious, and worked hard could succeed, for there was plenty of room to rise in American society. If he had

Andrew Carnegie is remembered for the billions of dollars (in today's money) he gave to build libraries, symphony halls, and many charities. Much of his wealth, unfortunately, was gained by exploiting the labor of tens of thousands of overworked and underpaid laborers.

done it, why not everybody else? By this theory, people who had not risen could only blame themselves, for they were probably lazy, thriftless, or perhaps simply incompetent. So far, Carnegie's "Gospel of Wealth" was much like Spencer's theory but Carnegie also said that people did not own their great wealth, but only held it in trust for the public: They must not lavish it on themselves, but use it to promote the public good. In his own life Carnegie gave the bulk of his vast fortune away to benefit the public.

The ideas of Spencer, Carnegie, and others grew out of the older eighteenth-century theory of *laissez-faire*. This is a French term that can be translated roughly as "hands-off"—in this case meaning that the government ought to stay out of business affairs, so the free-enterprise system can work according to its own laws, unfettered.

By the 1880s Spencer, in particular, was being widely read and discussed. His ideas were taken seriously by government officials, congressmen, and judges. Soon they found their way into America's highest law. One well-known example is the U.S. Supreme Court case of *Lochner v. New York* of 1905. The State of New York, to protect the health of workers, had passed a law limiting working hours in bakeries to no more than ten a day and sixty a week. A certain bakery owner employed his bakers for longer than ten hours and was prosecuted under the law. The case eventually reached the Supreme Court. In its decision the justices appealed to an idea nowhere found in the Constitution: the right of contract. The Court said that not only the bakery owner but the bakers as well had been deprived of property without due process of law—the property being the benefits they would gain from any contract they chose to make. Recall that the Fourteenth Amendment said that no state may deprive a person of property without due process of law. The justices said that the New York law limiting working hours in bakeries "necessarily interferes with the right of contract between employer and employees.... The act is not, within any fair meaning of the term, a health law, but is an illegal interference with the rights of individuals, both employers and employees to make contracts regarding labor upon such terms as they may think best . . ..”

The celebrated Justice Oliver Wendell Holmes Jr. dissented, saying governments in fact “interfere with the liberty to contract” in all sorts of laws about usury, Sunday store closings, and the like. “This case,” said Holmes, “is decided upon an economic theory which a large part of the country does not entertain . . .The Fourteenth Amendment does not enact Mr. Herbert Spencer’s *Social Statics.*” Holmes’s was a lonely voice in 1905, but later decisions of the Court did permit some state regulation of industry, and by the 1930s regulation by the U.S. government became routine.

At the time many people felt that there was a certain logic to the court’s reasoning. But others, like Justice Holmes, pointed out that the government certainly did interfere in the free workings of the competitive system when it suited the corporations. A major case was protective tariffs. These were taxes placed on foreign goods deliberately to keep their price up. Suppose an English manufacturer could sell woolen socks for 25¢ a pair, while the American manufacturer was less efficient and had to charge 30¢ a pair. People would of course buy the English socks. To prevent this, the government would put a tariff of, say, 10¢ a pair on foreign socks coming into the country. Now the English socks would cost 35¢ and could not compete with American ones.

Tariffs of this kind were placed on a whole array of goods. They had at first been justified by the need to encourage the growth of America’s “infant industries.” The effect, of course, was to keep the price of a great many goods higher than necessary, and it was the working people, who were scraping along as it was, who paid the price. Nor were they alone: Farmers earned their money from *exporting* products like wheat, corn, and tobacco. They had nothing to gain for import duties, which only made the things they had to buy more expensive. Of course, the industrialists pointed out that without the tariffs, they would go out of business, the laborers would lose their jobs, and the farmers would have no one to sell their wheat to. But the point is that the industrialists wanted no interference from the government, but they did want its help. It was a sort of double standard: laissez-faire when it regulates us; government involvement when it helps us.

In *Lochner* and other actions, the courts and many other government officials made it clear that they favored the corporations over industrial laborers. Why would the courts and other officials side with the corporation, against the majority of Americans, millions of whom were living in poverty? Some such officials honestly believed that the corporations were bringing great benefit to the United States; and it is certainly true that big business, through technological advances and efficient management, was increasing the material wealth of Americans in general, providing millions of jobs and countless consumer goods at cheap prices. In other instances government officials owned shares in corporations, and stood to benefit from high corporate profits. In yet other instances judges, legislators, and even congressmen were bribed by corporations to vote on their side. But in actuality, most middle-class Americans accepted laissez-faire policies and Spencer's justification for them. So many lived better than they had as children—better than their parents—that they believed the system was best for themselves and best for the nation. The poor would just have to work harder, and they, too, could rise to the middle class.

It must be said that the industrialists who became rich and powerful in the new industrial system were not all evil people intent on grinding down their workers to enrich themselves. During this period many of America's richest men gave millions, indeed billions in today's terms, to various causes, setting up foundations to improve medicine, support scientific research, and aid the poor, as well as building libraries and much more. The art in American museums, symphonies, and opera houses would not exist except for the money given by the wealthy of the post–Civil War period, which has been termed "The Gilded Age." But from a different perspective, it could be said that symphony halls were really paid for by the millions of workers who sweated and suffered to produce the wealth that the Carnegies and Rockefellers so lavishly gave away.

CHAPTER V

The Workers Fight Back

Many laboring people tended to accept as their natural fate the abuse they were suffering from the corporations; that is just the way things are, they assumed. However, a minority was prepared to stand up and make a fight of it. Back in Europe, the recent homeland of many workers in America's factories and mines, there had been growing up along with the industrial system a whole lot of ideas about the way labor was being treated by capital, that is, owners of the mines, factories, railroads, and such. All sorts of schemes were proposed to even things out, but the most important of them can be lumped under the heading of *socialism*.

Socialism has almost from the beginning had a bad name in the United States, partly because of its violation of private-property rights and partly because it is linked in people's minds with communism, which virtually all Americans have always opposed. Socialism has always been much more popular in Europe, where there have been socialist governments from time to time in many countries. Furthermore, although socialism is still unpopular in the United States, many of the ideas of the socialists of the late 1800s have become accepted institutions of

American life, like Social Security, Medicare, unemployment insurance, and more.

Only a small minority of immigrant workers (and a few old-stock Americans) believed in socialism, but they were likely to be active in organizing the workers against the industrial tycoons. Many laborers—not all, or even most of them Socialists—saw that the only chance that labor had against the power of the capitalists was by organizing unions. The labor union was not a new idea. Unions had existed in the late 1700s, and had even called strikes. By the 1830s the unions had managed to get the ten-hour workday in some types of work. But we must remember that in those days only a small minority of Americans worked in industrial jobs; unions could not effectively organize unskilled laborers. The successful unions of the period before the 1870s were made up of skilled craftsmen whose products were in demand and whose skills were not quickly mastered.

That changed with the rise of the industrial system, which by the later decades of the nineteenth century was employing over a third of American workers. The idea of unionizing spread and by 1870 there were many unions in America, like various Railway Brotherhoods, and the Ship Carpenters and Caulkers International. Through strikes, such unions occasionally were able to improve wages and hours, but their power remained small.

A key moment came in 1877. The country had been going through one of its periodic financial depressions. Employers had been cutting the wages of people who were already feeling desperate. In July, the Baltimore & Ohio Railroad cut wages by 10 percent.

The workers' response was swift. On July 16, 1877, Baltimore & Ohio workers in Martinsburg, West Virginia, struck. They refused to handle rail traffic, or let trains pass through the town. The president of the railroad asked West Virginia's governor for National Guard troops to open the railroad lines to traffic. Much to the dismay of the governor and

Because manufacturers were willing to use force against strikers, there was often violence. This picture shows the 6th regiment of the Maryland National Guard (center left) firing on strikers during the infamous railroad strike of 1877.

the railway officials, the troops at first mingled with the workers: The local militiamen had friends among the strikers. Nonetheless, later in the day a fight broke out and a railway worker who was guarding a switch was killed. Word of the death spread, deeply angering the workers, and everywhere throughout the entire Baltimore & Ohio system there were strikes. The line stopped operating. Workers gathered in Baltimore to carry their protests directly to the railway officials. There was a riot that

At Corning, New York, during the 1877 railroad strike, workers overturned whole trains so they could not be run by strikebreakers. Here, National Guardsmen hold strikers back while construction gangs right the overturned cars.

became a battle between workers and city police, leaving ten people dead and sixteen injured.

From the point of view of government officials, industrialists, and many of the middle class, the social system seemed to be breaking down. Maryland's governor, feeling that his state was on the verge of rebellion, asked President Rutherford B. Hayes to send in Federal troops. Hayes did so.

The idea that a president would use troops against his own citizens further enraged working people everywhere. Strikes and protests broke out along railroad lines in many cities, including Buffalo, New York, Reading, and Harrisburg, Pennsylvania. In Pittsburgh, railroad workers refused to allow rail traffic to pass through the city, which was an important industrial center, very much dependent on the railroads. Once again the state's government called up the militia; once again the local militiamen refused to take action against the strikers. The governor then called in militia from out of town and stationed them on trains. As the first train began to move slowly along the tracks, a crowd gathered to stop it. The soldiers fired, killing about twenty people and wounding seventy. The entire city of Pittsburgh erupted in a riot. The rioters tore into the Pennsylvania railroad yards, pulled up track, and burned buildings to the ground, destroying 104 locomotives and 2,153 railroad cars. Along the way another score of people were killed. Similar strikes and riots broke out in Chicago, St. Louis, Kansas City, Galveston, and San Francisco. It took two weeks for the fever to burn out; it was not until August that rail traffic was back to normal. Some fifty people had been killed, the railroads had lost $30 million. In turn they blackballed many of the strikers so they could no longer work in the railroad industry.

The great railroad strikes of 1877 shocked the nation. Many Americans felt that law and order were breaking down. It was now clear, in any case, that millions of workers deeply resented, indeed hated, the industrial system they found themselves trapped in. It was also clear that industrialists and corporation managers could count on city, state, and the Federal government to use troops against strikes, even to the point of killing strikers.

Nonetheless, workers continued to strike. In the first half of the 1880s there were on average 500 strikes a year; in the second half an average of a thousand; and in the 1890s an average of 1,300 involving a quarter of a million workers.

Furthermore, the union movement was growing. In 1878 a group called the Knights of Labor began its national activities. This was an order, secretly organized about ten years earlier, that included farmers and was as much a club as a union. At its peak in 1886 it had 700,000 members, and achieved some success in improving workers' conditions through strikes and other means. More significant was formation of the American Federation of Labor, led by Samuel Gompers. Born in England in 1850, he came to New York at thirteen, became a cigar maker, working amidst people who "ate, drank, and breathed Marxism and socialism." In 1886, Gompers helped to form the A.F. of L. He began by organizing skilled workers, who were not so easily replaced by strikebreakers, or "scabs," as they were called. Under Gompers' leadership the A.F. of L. grew in strength: By 1904 it had 1.7 million members, making it by far the strongest labor organization in America.

A second important union leader was Eugene Debs. Jailed for his part in a strike against the Pullman Palace Car Company in 1894 and discouraged by the use of troops against the workers, Debs came to believe that the whole system had to be changed. He helped to organize the American Socialist Party, which in theory would, if it ever gained power, turn control of industry over to the workers—or to the government in the workers' name. Debs ran for president—even once from jail—under the Socialist banner for many years, but, except in 1912 when he received 6 percent (nearly a million) never got more than a tiny fraction of the vote.

American workers called more than 20,000 strikes in the decades after the Civil War, most of them small, local, often spontaneous affairs. But some were nationwide. Three stand out in labor history. The first of these came in May of 1886, when a nationwide strike was called. Some 20,000 workers in many industries responded, closing down thousands of businesses large and small. As part of this general strike, a demonstration was called for May 3 in Chicago's Haymarket Square. Between 2,000 and 3,000 people were there. The meeting was peaceful, but as the crowd was dispersing a bomb exploded in the midst of a group of police-

One of the most important of all American labor leaders was Eugene Debs, who helped to organize the American Socialist Party, and was its presidential candidate during many campaigns.

men. Police began firing wildly into the crowd. When it was over, eight policemen and eight workers were dead, and another fifty people were wounded.

Once again the nation was shocked. The Chicago city and Illinois state governments decided to come down hard on "agitators" who were inciting working people to riot. They put on trial eight people thought to be radicals. It could not be shown that any of them had thrown the bomb or knew anything about it (to this day we do not know who threw the bomb); indeed, many of the eight could prove that they had not even been in Haymarket Square that evening. It did not matter: It was enough that they seemed to be radicals, and seven of them were sentenced to be executed. There were protests against this grossly unfair decision; nonetheless, in the end four of the men were hanged.

The second of these historic strikes came in 1892 at the Carnegie Steel Company plant in Homestead, near Pittsburgh. The workers there had a strong union, the Amalgamated Association of Iron, Steel, and Tin Workers. In 1892 the company tried to reduce wages and refused to recognize the union. The workers struck. Henry Clay Frick, the president of the company under Carnegie, brought in three hundred detectives from the Pinkerton Agency. The strikers fought the detectives in a famous gun battle and took over the plant, making it impossible for Frick to bring in strikebreakers. Once again the governor called out the militia. There was more shooting and many workers died. Eventually the strike failed. Frick fired the workers who had struck and brought in new ones.

The third historic strike involved the Pullman Company. At a time before airplanes, luxurious travel was by Pullman railway cars equipped with beds and even private rooms where the well-to-do could travel in

At the Homestead steel strike near Pittsburgh, strikers won a short-lived victory, forcing the hired Pinkerton men to surrender. This picture shows the Pinkerton men marching up a hill to the steel mill, guarded by armed strikers. However, Andrew Carnegie's assistant, Henry Clay Frick, brought in militia, who fired on the strikers, killing many, and the strike was ended.

comfort. The owner of the company, George Pullman, had built for his workers what seemed like a model town near Chicago. Surely this was a peaceable kingdom.

But it was not. In June of 1894, the country was once again in the midst of a financial depression. George Pullman decided to reduce wages. He did not, however, reduce the high rents he charged his workers to live in his model company houses. Caught in a squeeze, the workers called a strike. Pullman decided to fight. He refused to negotiate, believing that fees for the cars already out with the railroads would carry him through.

The workers appealed for help to the American Railway Union, led by Eugene Debs. The Union, to support the Pullman workers, shut down most of the American railroad system. The employers in turn got injunctions from the courts forbidding the strikes. They did so under a new law called the Sherman Antitrust Act. This law had been intended to prevent large corporations from joining together to set high prices. But the courts decided it could be used just as well to forbid workers from joining together to strike, thus acting "in restraint of trade." President Grover Cleveland sent in troops to enforce the injunction, declaring, "If it takes the entire Army and Navy of the United States to deliver a postal card in Chicago, that card will be delivered." There was fighting once again, deaths once again. Debs and some others were arrested and the strike collapsed. Pullman fired the workers who had struck the plants, brought in strikebreakers, and reopened for business.

These three cases suggest that the workers always lost the battles between management and labor. That was not so: The workers did indeed win some strikes. But with governors, judges, and even presidents willing to use troops against them, the odds were stacked. In most cases the workers lost. By the 1890s union leaders were growing cautious, trying to win small battles for limited gains, like small raises in pay, or slightly shorter hours. The use by American governments of troops against their own citizens is certainly a black mark on American history.

Government officials tended to side with the manufacturers against the workers, whom they sometimes saw as unruly mobs upsetting law and order. President Grover Cleveland brought in troops against strikers— and he was not the only official to do so.

We must remember, however, that union members have never been a majority of workers in the United States, and in the period we are studying it is unlikely that they ever exceeded 5 percent of the industrial workforce. (Membership reached about 15 percent during World War I and peaked at about 34 percent in the mid-1950s.) Of course many non-union workers supported union ideas, and were willing to go on strike, even to fight police and soldiers. Even so, the majority of workers, fearful of losing their jobs, tended to accept the abuses of the industrial situation and do the best they could to get along. Indeed, most middle-class Americans believed that the government was right to use force to put down strikes. Nonetheless, the use of troops to intimidate workers put governments on the side of the great industrial corporations in a way that would not be tolerated today.

CHAPTER VI

Government Starts to Regulate Industry

Despite the strong inclination of government officials to give the corporations free rein, there were a lot of Americans who believed that big business was taking advantage of the situation and running roughshod over too many people. Farm families, still 40 percent of the American population, believed they were suffering from exorbitant railroad rates, and from protective tariffs favorable to business. Small businessmen thought that government policies favored the huge industrial firms. Laboring people had very good reason for seeking greater government control of the corporations. Other Americans were upset by seeing government troops killing strikers.

Yet there was a question of how far any government could go in putting restraints on the corporations. The Constitution gave the national government the power to "regulate commerce . . . among the several states." The legal question was always how to distinguish which businesses were in *interstate commerce* and thus under Congress's authority, and which businesses were in *intrastate* commerce subject only to state government regulation.

The railroads, clearly, were engaged in interstate commerce. On these

New technologies, like the Bessemer process for producing high-quality steel, dramatically increased the wealth of America. But as such industries were consolidated into a few massive companies, many people began to worry that the corporations were gaining too much control of the American economy. Here, workers in a Bessemer plant pour steel.

grounds the Supreme Court struck down state laws regulating railroads: Only the Federal government could pass such laws. Many congressmen came from farming areas and were sensitive to farmers' interests, and in 1887 Congress passed the Interstate Commerce Act, which set up an Interstate Commerce Commission. At first the Interstate Commerce Commission was a rather weak body, which could do little more than investigate problems and make recommendations. The few regulations it did put in place, such as outlawing pools and rebates, were quickly undercut by courts unsympathetic to government regulation. But the Interstate Commerce Act was important, because for the first time— exactly one hundred years after the U.S. Constitution was written—it put into effect the idea that the Federal government had constitutional authority, indeed a duty, to regulate private businesses for the public good.

But there was still a considerable feeling in the nation that something more had to be done. Everybody—farmers, workers, government officials, the middle class, and even small businessmen—was troubled by the *consolidation* of many industries into a handful of trusts or other arrangements that left control of essential industries in the hands of a few people. Not only were major industries dominated by a few trusts; so were many minor ones, like the National Linseed Oil Trust, organized in 1885, and the distillers and cattle feeders' trusts set up two years later. Too much power was in too few hands, many felt. Even President Cleveland, who had sent troops in to break the Pullman strike, said in 1888 that the people were being "trampled to death beneath the iron heel" of the trusts.

Thus in the 1880s a number of states passed antitrust laws of various kinds, setting limits on their powers and making certain kinds of business practices illegal. But most of the trusts were national corporations, with factories in many states, and customers everywhere. They were engaged in interstate commerce, and could only be controlled by the Federal government. For two years Congress debated. Finally, in 1890, it passed what became known as the Sherman Antitrust Act.

The act declared illegal "every contract, combination in the form of a trust or otherwise, or conspiracy, in restraint of trade or commerce among the several States, or with foreign nations." It provided fines and jail terms for those who broke the law.

In fact, the Sherman Antitrust Act was far weaker than it seemed, and it was made even weaker by the Supreme Court in cases brought under it. In one such case the Supreme Court ruled that a monopoly in sugar *refining* was not *commerce*, which had to do only with buying, selling, and transporting—as though companies could refine sugarcane without buying or selling it. In another case it said that a conspiracy had to be proven: If a monopoly came about by the natural workings of the marketplace, it was not illegal. Again, the Congress had left it to the courts to define terms like "restraint of trade," and "combination," and the courts again and again chose to side with big business. Not suprisingly, after it was clear that the Supreme Court was going to interpret the Sherman Antitrust Act in a way favorable to business, a great many industries were consolidated, many more—ironically—than before the act was passed. Corporations that could be brought to court for arranging pools and trusts, for the most part, found themselves safe from government suit if they just merged into one big company. It would be twenty-four years before Congress put teeth into the Sherman Antitrust Act. But the act was nonetheless important, for once again it said flatly that the government had a right and duty to set limits on what business could and could not do. The good of the public had to be considered; private enterprise with its central profit motive was too likely to put profits first and public interest second if it was left unrestrained.

Yet this idea, that corporations had to take the public interest into account in doing business, was not accepted by industrialists and many others. As late as 1913, a judge ruling in a lawsuit involving the celebrated car maker Henry Ford said flatly, "A business corporation is organized and carried on primarily for the profit of the stockholders." Under the American system of private free-enterprise capitalism, the profit motive is what keeps the economy going. But fair competition makes it work for everyone; when competition is undercut by monopoly, then the government steps in with regulations like the Interstate Commerce Act

Henry Ford was one of the first to develop the mass-production system of making automobiles. He believed that corporations ought to concern themselves with the public good, but he also said flatly that they also had to be concerned about showing a profit for the shareholders. Here he is in 1946 posing in a car he first operated in 1896.

(repealed in 1996) and the Sherman Antitrust Act (still on the books).

Whatever the rights and wrongs of the industrial system that was created in the years between the end of the Civil War and 1900 or so, there is no question that it had vastly increased the amount of things available to Americans. In that sense, the United States had become, by 1900, the most prosperous nation in the history of the world. Many argued—and still argue today—that a great many of the products available were frivolous gewgaws, and that Americans were far too concerned with buying things at the expense of other more emotionally satisfying activities. Nonetheless, the industrial machine did bring, along with the torrent of gewgaws, a lot of things that made life easier and more comfortable for Americans of every degree of poverty or wealth.

For Americans in 1900, the world had changed. People in middle age at the turn of the century could remember a time when most things they had were made or grown at home or in a nearby village or town. Vegetables came from the backyard garden, clothes were cut and sewn by Mom and Sis, a new bureau was made by the cabinetmaker in the next town. Now, in 1900, vegetables came by refrigerated railroad car from California and Florida, clothes from textile factories in Boston and New York, furniture from North Carolina and Michigan. These middle-aged people had seen electric lighting, telephones, washing machines, hot water that came from a faucet instead of a tub on the stove, heat from a coal furnace in the cellar come into their homes.

The new products flowing out of the industrial machine were going everywhere across the United States, carried by the vast, quick railroad system. Water tumblers from Pittsburgh, sheet music from Cincinnati, and shirts from New York were being used in Charleston, St. Louis, and San Francisco. The marketplace was the whole nation, and the American family that moved, as so many did, from the East Coast cities to the Midwest or farther, would find familiar brands of water tumblers, shirts, and nearly everything else wherever they went. Indeed, American industry could produce far more consumer products than people knew about or wanted. By the 1890s the problem was no longer how to manufacture enough, but how to sell the billions of items pouring from factories all across the nation. And thus a new industry arose: advertising.

Ads to sell land, wine, books, and cloth had appeared in newspapers as far back as colonial days. With the advent of high-speed presses and other improvements in printing, the amount of advertising in periodicals increased. But it really boomed with the coming of the mass-produced goods pouring out of the new industrial machine after 1880.

Magazines still existing today, like *Cosmopolitian*, *Good Housekeeping*, and *Town and Country*, were started in the last decades of the nineteenth century, and their circulation soared to 64 million by 1905. By that time it was abundantly clear that American industry could turn out more soap, chocolate, and pianos than Americans thought they needed. Businesses realized that they had to use advertising to persuade Americans that their brand of soap or chocolate was somehow superior to all the others—or indeed was necessary at all. As one historian of the

These early advertisements were lighthearted, humorous and very colorful. By the 1890s advertisers were already using sophisticated methods to attract customers.

Many advertisements made ludicrous, even dangerous, claims. This ad touts bitters as a "certain cure" for malaria and a host of other diseases. Eventually some curbs were put on advertisements of this kind.

advertising industry puts it, advertising was necessary to get people to buy, "not to satisfy their own fundamental needs, but rather to satisfy the real, historic needs of capitalistic productive machinery." People had to be persuaded that they needed things they had never thought they needed before—even that they had never heard of before.

Advertising today is so much a part of our lives that like the air around us, we hardly realize we are breathing it in. It has been estimated that average American children see some 20,000 television advertisements alone before they grow up. The questions of how these messages affect young minds have been much debated by experts. While many people agree that constantly telling young children that they ought to acquire things cannot help but make them more materialistic, with the exception of tobacco and liquor, there has not been any strong outcry against advertising from the American public.

But even by 1900 there was beginning to be debate over the control exerted by manufacturers over advertising media, in those days mainly magazines and newspapers. Most of the money to pay for such publications came not from the pennies readers paid for them but the money manufacturers paid to advertise in them. Needless to say, editors of magazines and newspapers were loath to run stories criticizing products that might be advertised in them, even when they knew such products were bad for people. But a time came when some editors grew "disgusted by the deceptive and false claims for patent medicines," and some magazines stopped accepting these and similar ads. Ever since, there have been occasional attempts by governments to crack down on false advertising, most notably the campaign against tobacco promotion at the end of the twentieth century.

It is a simple truth that most advertising media in 1900, as is the case today, get most of their money from a relatively small number of large corporations in industries like food, soap and cleaning supplies, food and beverages, and automobiles. Without the advertisers, the magazines, newspapers, and television programs would not exist. But, of course, in many ways the advertisers can determine what we see and read—and often do. That is the trade-off.

Along with advertising came new methods of retailing the enormous outpouring of goods. New companies selling by mail, like Sears Roebuck, sent out free millions of fat mail-order catalogues offering an array of goods ranging from shirts to trombones, pitchforks to books. Once again, these mail-order companies were supplying Americans everywhere with the same brand of pitchforks and same book titles.

So were the chain stores. The most famous of them were the Woolworth "Five and Ten Cent" stores, which boasted that they sold nothing for more than a dime. There were many others besides Woolworth's, the forerunners of the great national chains we are so familiar with today, like Sears Roebuck, Wal-Mart, and Burger King.

Mass-circulation magazines, the forerunner of today's vast media system, were started in the nineteenth century. Here are two early magazines still being published. At left, Vogue *for 1911; at right,* Ladies Home Journal *for 1913.*

The problem, as it had been from the moment the industrial machine began to rise in the nation, was that this prosperity was very unevenly spread. The *majority* of Americans simply were not getting their fair share. The laborers in the factories, mines, driving wagons, guiding the canal boats, were, in 1900, working long hours for low wages and living pinched lives in crowded and unsanitary conditions. Their attempts to improve conditions for themselves through unions and strikes had run into the combined power of government and the large corporations that employed so many of them.

Farmers too, in 1900, were suffering. Overproduction of many products, like wheat and corn, had driven prices down, and the railroads were scooping off much of the small profits that remained. In 1900 many farmers were worse off than they had been in 1870.

These problems did not correct themselves. Only slowly, after 1900, did governments, bit by bit, attack the suffering of workers and farmers by limiting hours, setting minimum wages, putting through building codes and sanitary laws that, for example, required landlords to install heat, running water, and fire escapes in tenement buildings. Unions, too, slowly increased in strength, in part from new laws meant to aid them. In the 1930s, when the country was sunk into a Depression so bad that many felt the whole free-enterprise system was going under, the government under President Franklin D. Roosevelt pushed through a number of laws to aid workers in their fight for better conditions. However, not until after World War II, when the Depression was over, did the benefits of the new industrial system finally begin to be shared by everybody. It had been more than a hundred years since the rise of the railroads began the creation of the great American industrial system. But perhaps it always takes a long time for a society to come to terms with a change as sweeping as this one was. For all the miseries that came with the rise of the industrial economy, it would be hard to find anyone today who would want to go back to the way things were in 1870.

BIBLIOGRAPHY

For Students

Adair, Gene. *Thomas Alva Edison: Inventing the Electric Age.* New York: Oxford, 1996. Grades 7+.

Altman, Linda Jacobs. *The Pullman Strike of 1894: Turning Point for American Labor.* Brookfield, Conn.: Millbrook Press, 1994.

Bowman, John S. *Andrew Carnegie: Steel Tycoon.* Englewood Cliffs, N.J.: Silver Burdett, 1989.

Brown, Gene. *The Struggle to Grow: Expansionism and Industrialization, 1880–1913.* New York: 21st Century Books, 1993.

Buranelli, Vincent. *Thomas Alva Edison.* Englewood Cliffs, N.J.: Silver Burdett, 1989. Grades 5–7.

Clark, Judith Freeman. *America's Gilded Age: An Eyewitness History.* New York: Facts on File, 1992.

Colman, Penny. *Strike! The Bitter Struggle of American Workers from Colonial Times to the Present.* Brookfield, Conn.: Millbrook Press, 1995.

Freedman, Russell. *Kids at Work: Lewis Hine and the Crusade Against Child Labor.* New York: Clarion Books, 1994.

Greene, Laura Offenhartz. *Child Labor: Then and Now.* New York: Franklin Watts, 1992.

Meltzer, Milton. *Bread—and Roses: The Struggle of American Labor, 1865-1915.* New York: Facts on File, 1990.

Parker, Steve. *Thomas Edison and Electricity.* New York: Chelsea House, 1995. Grades 4–8.

Ravage, Barbara. *George Westinghouse: A Genius for Invention.* Austin, Texas.: Raintree-Stack-Vaughn Pubs., 1997.

Sherrow, Victoria. *The Triangle Factory Fire.* Brookfield, Conn.: Millbrook Press, 1995.

For Teachers

Baldwin, Neil. *Edison: Inventing the Century.* New York: Hyperion, 1995.

Bruchey, Stuart. *Growth of the Modern American Economy.* New York: Dodd, Mead and Co., 1975.

Cochran, Thomas G. and William Miller. *The Age of Enterprise: A Social History of Industrial America.* New York: Macmillan Company, 1992.

Dubofsky, Melvin. *Industrialism and the American Worker, 1865–1920.* 2nd ed. Arlington Heights, Ill.: Harlan Davidson, 1996.

Heilbroner, Robert. *The Economic Transformation.* 4th ed. New York: Harcourt Brace Jovanovich, 1998.

Kirkland, Edward. *Industry Comes of Age: Business, Labor, and Public Policy, 1860–1897.* New York: Hill and Wang, 1989.

Laurie, Bruce. *Artisans into Workers: Labor in Nineteenth-Century America.* New York: Hill and Wang, 1989.

Licht, Walter. *Industrializing America: The Nineteenth Century.* Baltimore: Johns Hopkins Press, 1995.

Mayer, Martin. *Madison Avenue, U.S.A.* Lincolnwood, Ill.: NTC Contemporary Publishing, 1994.

Millard, A. J. *Edison and the Business of Innovation.* Baltimore: Johns Hopkins Press, 1990.

Montgomery, David. *Citizen Worker: The Experience of Workers in the United States with Democracy and the Free Market During the Nineteenth Century.* New York: Cambridge University Press, 1994.

Oliver, John W. *History of American Technology.* New York: The Ronald Press, 1956.

Porter, Glenn. *The Rise of Big Business, 1865–1920.* 2nd ed. Arlington Heights, Ill.: Harlan Davidson, 1992.

Rayback, Joseph G. *A History of American Labor.* New York: The Free Press, 1966.

Rosenzweig, Roy. *Eight Hours for What We Will: Workers and Leisure in an Industrial City, 1870–1920.* New York: Cambridge University Press, 1985.

INDEX

Page numbers for illustrations are in **boldface**.

cattle industry, 31
Caulkers International, 64
charity, 61–62
Chicago, 68–69, 71
children, 50, 52, 54, 80
cities, 11, 26–27, 46
Cleveland, Grover, 71, **72**, 75
Cleveland, Ohio, 43–44
clothing, 9, 41. *See also* garment
    industry
coal, 15, 16, 49
communication, 17
competition, 30, 36–40, **37**, 56,
    76
consumer products, 77–78
contract, right of, 59–60
copper industry, 31
Corning, New York, **66**
corporations
    advantages, 34–35
    and advertising, 81
    and competition, 38–40
    development, 32–34, **33**
    Ford's view of, 76
    immortality, 35
    Supreme Court rulings, 35–36
corruption, 27, 30–31, 42, 61
counties, 26

Darwin, Charles, 56
Debs, Eugene, 68, **69**, 71
depressions, 50, 83
derailments, 20
DeWitt Clinton, **25**
Drake, Edwin L., 16, 43, **44**

economic crises, 50, 83
economies of scale, 40
Edison, Thomas Alva, 18, **19**
education, 43, 50, 54
    Spencer's theory, 57
electricity, 18–19, 22
England
    and railroads, 23
    and steam engine, 14
    and steel, 15–16
    textile industry, 12
entrepreneurs
    attitude of, 22
    as robber barons, 41–42
    and steel, 16
ethics, 38
Europe, and socialism, 63–64

factories
    earliest modern, 13
    rural versus urban, 15
farm equipment, 40
farmers
    and overproduction, 83
    and railroads, 29, 73–74, 83
farms, 9, **11**
fire, **53**
Fitch, John, 14, **14**
Ford, Henry, 76, **77**
Fourteenth Amendment, 35–36,
    59–60
Franklin, Benjamin, 18
free enterprise
    and competition, 36, 76
    and government's role, 59

transportation *(Continued)*
    pre- and post-railroad, 23–24
    rebates, 43–44
    steamships, 14, **14**
Triangle Shirtwaist factory, 53
trusts, 38–40, 75–76

unemployment, 50–51
unemployment insurance, 51
unions, 64, 67–72, 83
U.S. Rubber, 40
U.S. Steel, 39
urbanization, 11, 41

Vanderbilt, Cornelius, 45, **46**, 47
Virginia, railroads in, 24

wages
    from industrialist's view, 48
    minimum, 35–36, 83
    for skilled workers, 54
    Supreme Court ruling, 35–36
    typical, 50–51
    and unions, 64
    for women, 51

Waterbury, Connecticut, 49
Watt, James, 24, **24**
wealth, 56, 59, 82
welding machine, 22
Westinghouse, George, 18, 19–22
Westinghouse Co., 39–40
"white collar" workers, 40–41, **42**
Wilkes-Barre, Pennsylvania, 31
women
    in 1870, 9–10
    African-American, 51–52
    in mills, 13, 15
    in workplace, 51, 53
work. *See also* wages
    and African-Americans, 51–52
    after industrialization, 11, 50
    and children, 50
    conditions of, 35–36, 40–41, **49**,
        49–50, 52–53, **53**, 82–83
in corporations, 32, **33**, 46
before industrialization, 9, 50
workday, 49, 59–60
workers, 54, **55**, 64. *See also* labor

JAMES LINCOLN COLLIER is the author of a number of books both for adults and for young people, including the social history *The Rise of Selfishness in America*. He is also noted for his biographies and historical studies in the field of jazz. Together with his brother, Christopher Collier, he has written a series of award-winning historical novels for children widely used in schools, including the Newbery Honor classic, *My Brother Sam Is Dead*. A graduate of Hamilton College, he lives with his wife in New York City.

CHRISTOPHER COLLIER grew up in Fairfield County, Connecticut and attended public schools there. He graduated from Clark University in Worcester, Massachusetts and earned M.A. and Ph.D. degrees at Columbia University in New York City. After service in the Army and teaching in secondary schools for several years, Mr. Collier began teaching college in 1961. He is now Professor of History at the University of Connecticut and Connecticut State Historian. Mr. Collier has published many scholarly and popular books and articles about Connecticut and American history. With his brother, James, he is the author of nine historical novels for young adults, the best known of which is *My Brother Sam Is Dead*. He lives with his wife Bonnie, a librarian, in Orange, Connecticut.